Spot the Differences

Crow or Raven?

by Jamie Rice

Bullfrog Books

Ideas for Parents and Teachers

Bullfrog Books let children practice reading informational text at the earliest reading levels. Repetition, familiar words, and photo labels support early readers.

Before Reading

- Discuss the cover photo. What does it tell them?

- Look at the picture glossary together. Read and discuss the words.

Read the Book

- "Walk" through the book and look at the photos. Let the child ask questions. Point out the photo labels.

- Read the book to the child, or have him or her read independently.

After Reading

- Prompt the child to think more. Ask: What did you know about crows and ravens before reading this book? What more would you like to learn?

Bullfrog Books are published by Jump!
5357 Penn Avenue South
Minneapolis, MN 55419
www.jumplibrary.com

Copyright © 2023 Jump! International copyright reserved in all countries. No part of this book may be reproduced in any form without written permission from the publisher.

Library of Congress Cataloging-in-Publication Data

Names: Rice, Jamie, author.
Title: Crow or raven? / by Jamie Rice.
Description: Minneapolis, MN: Jump!, Inc., [2023]
Series: Spot the differences | Includes index.
Audience: Ages 5–8
Identifiers: LCCN 2022011723 (print)
LCCN 2022011724 (ebook)
ISBN 9798885241526 (hardcover)
ISBN 9798885241533 (paperback)
ISBN 9798885241540 (ebook)
Subjects: LCSH: Crows—Juvenile literature.
Corvus corax—Juvenile literature.
Classification: LCC QL696.P2367 R53 2023 (print)
LCC QL696.P2367 (ebook) | DDC 598.8/64—dc23/eng/20220401
LC record available at https://lccn.loc.gov/2022011723
LC ebook record available at https://lccn.loc.gov/2022011724

Editor: Katie Chanez
Designer: Emma Bersie

Photo Credits: Eric Isselee/Shutterstock, cover (left), 1 (right), 20 (right); Valentin Mosichev/Shutterstock, cover (right); Vishnevskiy Vasily/Shutterstock, 1 (left); Tierfotoagentur/Alamy, 3, 14–15, 21 (left), 23bl; Gerald A. DeBoer/Shutterstock, 4; Elvis01/Shutterstock, 5; Judy Kennamer/Dreamstime, 6–7 (top); Tom Reichner/Shutterstock, 6–7 (bottom); Zoonar GmbH/Alamy, 8–9, 23tl; Frank Lane Picture Agency/SuperStock, 10–11, 23bm; Duncan Usher/Minden Pictures/SuperStock, 12–13, 23tr; 54613/Shutterstock, 15 (top), 23tm; Daniela Pelazza/Shutterstock, 15 (bottom), 23br; RCKeller/iStock, 16–17; Mauro Toccaceli/Alamy, 18–19; retofuerst/Shutterstock, 20 (left), 24 (top); Rosa Jay/Shutterstock, 21 (right); Oksana Kuznetsova Dnepr/Shutterstock, 22 (left); Risto Puranen/Shutterstock, 22 (right); Farinosa/iStock, 24 (bottom).

Printed in the United States of America at Corporate Graphics in North Mankato, Minnesota.

Table of Contents

Fly High!... 4

See and Compare... 20

Quick Facts.. 22

Picture Glossary.. 23

Index 24

To Learn More.. 24

How to Use This Book

In this book, you will see pictures of both crows and ravens. Can you tell which one is in each picture?

Hint: You can find the answers if you flip the book upside down!

Fly High!

This is a crow.

This is a raven.

5

Both birds are black.

They look the same.

But they are not.

How?

Let's see!

Both have feathers.

A crow's neck feathers are flat.

A raven's are fluffy.

Which is this?

Answer: raven

feathers

beak

Both have beaks.

A crow's is straight and thin.

A raven's is curved and thick.

Which is this?

Look up!
Both birds fly.
A crow flaps its wings.
A raven soars.
Which is this?

Answer: crow

wing

tail

A crow's tail is like a fan.
A raven's is like a wedge.
It ends in a point.
Which is this?

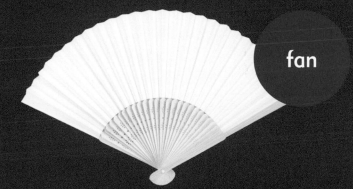

fan

wedge

Crows fly in groups.
Ravens fly in pairs.
Which are these?

Answer: ravens

Crows often live in cities.

Ravens do not.

Which is this?

Answer: crow

See and Compare

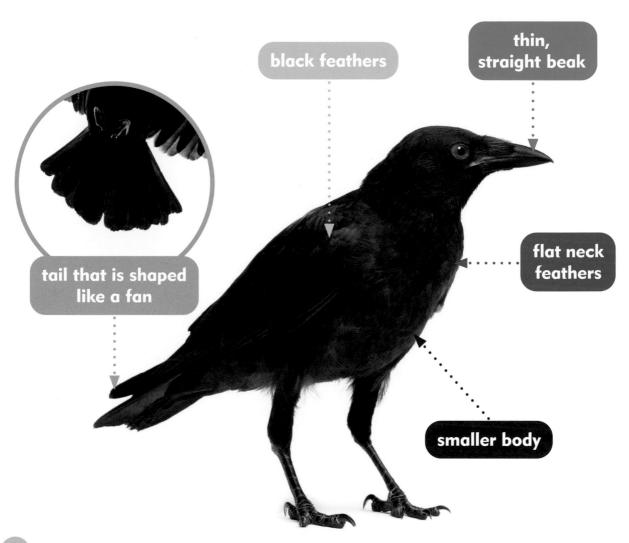

black feathers

thin, straight beak

flat neck feathers

tail that is shaped like a fan

smaller body

20

black feathers

thick, curved beak

tail that is shaped like a wedge

fluffy neck feathers

larger body

21

Quick Facts

Crows and ravens are both birds with black feathers. They eat meat, insects, and fruit. They raise their young in nests. They are similar, but they have differences. Take a look!

Crows

- often live in cities and towns
- make cawing sounds
- eat more fruit, nuts, and insects
- wings up to three feet (0.9 meters) across

Ravens

- rarely seen in cities or towns
- make croaking sounds
- eat more meat, such as mice and baby tortoises
- wings up to four feet (1.2 meters) across

Picture Glossary

curved
Bent or rounded.

fan
An object that is used to wave air on yourself.

flaps
Moves up and down.

soars
Flies or hovers high in the air.

straight
Without a curve or bend.

wedge
An object that is thin and pointed at one end and thick at the other.

Index

beaks 11

cities 19

fan 15

feathers 8

flaps 12

fly 12, 16

groups 16

pairs 16

soars 12

tail 15

wedge 15

wings 12

To Learn More

Finding more information is as easy as 1, 2, 3.

❶ Go to www.factsurfer.com

❷ Enter "croworraven?" into the search box.

❸ Choose your book to see a list of websites.